LIVING IN A

BUDDHIST

MONASTERY

By Robin Twiddy

LIFE
LONG AGO

BookLife
PUBLISHING

©2021

BookLife Publishing Ltd.
King's Lynn
Norfolk PE30 4LS

ISBN: 978-1-83927-467-1

Written by:
Robin Twiddy

Edited by:
Emilie Dufresne

Designed by:
Danielle Webster-Jones

A catalogue record for this book
is available from the British
Library.

All facts, statistics, web addresses
and URLs in this book were
verified as valid and accurate at
time of writing. No responsibility
for any changes to external
websites or references can be
accepted by either the author
or publisher.

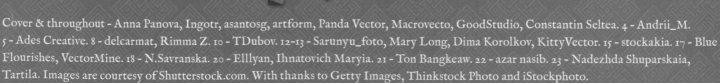

IMAGE CREDITS

Cover & throughout - Anna Panova, Ingotr, asantosg, artform, Panda Vector, Macrovecto, GoodStudio, Constantin Seltea. 4 - Andrii_M.
5 - Ades Creative. 8 - delcarmat, Rimma Z. 10 - TDubov. 12-13 - Sarunyu_foto, Mary Long, Dima Korolkov, KittyVector. 15 - stockakia. 17 - Blue
Flourishes, VectorMine. 18 - N.Savranska. 20 - Elllyan, Ihnatovich Maryia. 21 - Ton Bangkeaw. 22 - azar nasib. 23 - Nadezhda Shuparskaia,
Tartila. Images are courtesy of Shutterstock.com. With thanks to Getty Images, Thinkstock Photo and iStockphoto.

CONTENTS

Words that look like THIS can be found in the glossary on page 24.

WELCOME *to the* MONASTERY

Hi, my name is Jampa. I am a Buddhist monk. That means that I study and learn from the teachings of the Buddha. He was a very WISE man who lived a long time ago.

Jampa is a Tibetan Buddhist monk. There have been MONASTERIES in Tibet for over 1,200 years.

I work and live in the monastery. If I study hard enough, I can become a lama. Lamas are great <u>SPIRITUAL</u> leaders. Buddhist monks work towards <u>ENLIGHTENMENT</u> – I'll tell you more about this later!

I hit this gong to tell the other monks that it is time to get up and go to morning prayer.

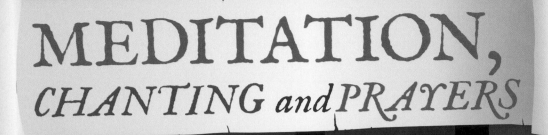

MEDITATION, *CHANTING and* PRAYERS

Everyone comes together for meditation. We meditate to help us be more <u>MINDFUL</u> and make our minds strong. Today I will be meditating on my breath and paying attention to how I breathe in and out.

Meditating can be concentrating on one thing, or just noticing where your mind goes.

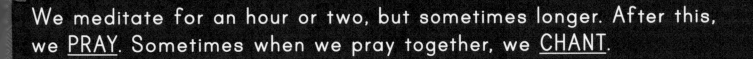

We meditate for an hour or two, but sometimes longer. After this, we PRAY. Sometimes when we pray together, we CHANT.

Buddhist monks do a lot for others. They pray to help people in need around the world.

Collecting ALMS

We go to visit the people in the village. The people show <u>RESPECT</u> to us by giving us food. This is called alms.

Alms are gifts that help the monks to live their life in the monastery.

8

The main type of alms is food. In return for alms, we pray for the people in the village and guide them on how to live a good Buddhist life.

People give alms to show us thanks. We spend our lives learning and teaching about the Buddha, when they cannot.

BREAKFAST

While the other monks are still chanting and praying, I will bring out breakfast with my friends. The monks will drink yak's milk and eat while they finish praying.

This is how we do things at our monastery, but other monasteries might do things a bit differently.

Breakfast is usually a type of flatbread or oatmeal. We don't eat in the afternoon or evening so it's important to have a good breakfast.

I like flatbread. Sometimes I even help make it.

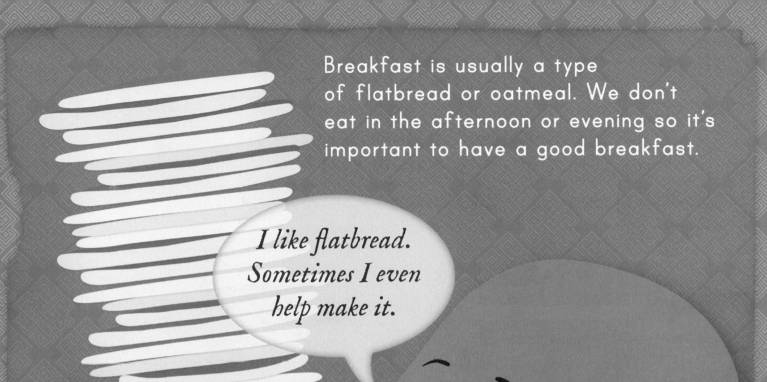

CHORES

Now I need to carry out my chores. These might be cleaning, sweeping, or doing laundry, but they are different in each monastery.

Today I am sweeping the courtyard, but my chores could be anything that helps to keep the monastery clean and working.

Tomorrow I might be helping in the kitchens or fixing something such as that broken door.

LUNCH

Now it's lunchtime. We have our lunch before midday and we only eat food that is <u>IN SEASON</u>. We have something light that will keep our body healthy.

We believe that food that is in season is the best food for our bodies at that time.

We all eat together but we don't talk. We focus on the food on our plates, and chew slowly and carefully. After lunch, we won't eat again until breakfast.

We are being mindful about how we eat!

AFTERNOON PRAYER

After lunch, we pray again. We repeat our mantras so many times that we learn them off by heart. I am using prayer beads to count how many mantras I have repeated.

A mantra is a phrase or sentence that a Buddhist concentrates on to help them pray.

Mantras often contain the teachings of the Buddha. They help us to try to be more like the Buddha and work towards enlightenment.

LESSONS

We meet with our masters to study the Buddhist TEXTS and to learn the Tibetan language. We also learn all about the Buddha's life.

The Buddha was a prince called Siddhartha who gave up all his money and power when he saw how much people were suffering.

Siddhartha spent a long time meditating until he reached enlightenment. Then he taught others how to become <u>ENLIGHTENED</u>, too.

For the Buddha, being enlightened means understanding why people suffer and breaking free of the wheel of <u>REINCARNATION</u>.

MEDITATION

In the evenings, I sometimes meditate on the teachings of the Buddha. I will sit very still and think about the Buddha's life and teachings and how I can use them in my own life.

'Buddha' means 'enlightened'.

I am going to keep meditating and learning about the Buddha's teachings as I make my own path on the journey to enlightenment.

BEDTIME

Finally, the day is over. It has been a long day, but after meditation it is time for bed. I hope you have enjoyed visiting this monastery.

Tomorrow will be much like today, but I can continue my journey to enlightenment and understand more about the world.

Kha-leh shu. That means goodbye in Tibetan.

GLOSSARY

chant   say or sing words over and over in a rhythm

enlightened   the point where someone has gained wisdom and understanding about the world

enlightenment   the highest level of spiritual growth and understanding in Buddhism

in season   grown and ready to eat in the current season

mindful   to be aware of what is happening around you

monasteries   the buildings used by a community of monks

pray   to thank or talk to a spiritual being

reincarnation   the belief that we are reborn into new bodies after death

respect   to think very highly of someone

spiritual   to do with the soul or spirit rather than the physical world

texts   books or writings, often very important

wise   having good judgement

INDEX

24